Distillations

Distillations
New Poems

by

E. Smith Dunlap

REGENT PRESS
Berkeley, California

[paperback]
ISBN 13: 978-1-58790-645-9
ISBN 10: 1-58790-645-7

Library of Congress Catelog Number: *forthcoming*

All photos by the author.

Manufactured in the U.S.A.

REGENT PRESS
Berkeley, California
www.regentpress.net

Contents

Foreword for *Distillations*

by Nina Diamond

Silver linings exist, but they can be elusive. We get tangled up, lost and tired. Thankfully, this book is a useful tool. *Distillations* burnishes the gleam on even quotidian objects and moments. Like the author, these poems are unabashedly curious, hearty, and wise.

When Elaine and I met one summer 35 years ago, these qualities were immediately apparent. She was 40, a college professor, and I was 19. We were both starry-eyed and masochistic enough to enroll in an intensive language course: A year of Ancient Greek in 10 weeks. On day three, I got extremely sick. When I resurfaced, I was already damned – like Orpheus sneaking a look at Eurydice. Before dropping out, I endured weeks of shame and despair during which the silver lining began blessedly, to emerge: Elaine and I had now become friends.

Over the years, I'd like to believe I've learned a great deal from her. She says, "I have worked at beauty," and now these poems are her proxies, enabling us to appreciate what's often obscured. Her discernment grows from a uniquely open and optimistic sensibility. Her writing is grounded in wide-reaching scholarship and unbounded enthusiasm that spans literature, visual arts, food, music, science, and travel. Her perspective is not precious or exclusionary, but generous, illuminating shared human awareness, "sometimes/We slip into history/With a substantial jolt."

This relationship to history is keenly personal and frankly, wild. Meet Clytemnestra. Admittedly she "killed the S.O.B.," but here she's presented more empathetically: "Perhaps she tried/To turn to gardening." In Elaine's world, mythical people, especially women, are nuanced in the way of people we actually know. Maybe Orpheus didn't abandon Eurydice on the trek out of Hades, but the other way around? Even ordinary moments can have cosmic reverberations. Hamlet and the sub-atomic universe are in her morning coffee. A garden door swings between chance and choice.

These poems move us through space and time, from Bhutan to Berkeley. The natural world often provides a conduit. During an eclipse, she has one foot in Ancient Greece, howling at the moon. On the streets of her beloved London, she thinks back to the centuries when they were "All bonneted and booted/ And unfair," through to the present pandemic, and forward to crowds yet unborn. "How will they ever meet/Or marry/Or have children?" she wonders. "We come for history/And fail to see/That we are making and apart/Of what is now and yet to be."

What you'll read in this book are toasts to life, short and bold. The lines bubble up off the page. She catches our eye over the top of the glass, and suddenly we land somewhere else surprising and expansive. In "At This Moment," there's a spin around the world's chaos and destruction, but at the end she confides, "And I am about to take a bath." Inside a temple in the Himalayas, the circling path of an old, hunched woman is ultimately revealed to be "mine."

"Every essence has its use," she writes, and there's a lot to pack in: Byzantine columns, Higgs bosun, Bartok. References are loose and casual. Homer here, T.S. Eliot and his peaches there. A poem for Seamus Heaney's death is accompanied by a photo of a melting iceberg. Both giants glisten, disappearing. There's much cross-pollination: family and fury, Dante to Dylan. I saw this on my first visit to her home. I was stopped in my tracks by the riot of art, textiles, and talismans from all over the globe. She laughed at me. "The cave of the wizard is not bare," she said. These poems could not coalesce without her first having taken in the wonder of the constellations.

Elaine has taken her time to publish this book, but her timing is good. Her memory is ripe. As she writes, "My shelves are full/Stocked with experience/Bought with choices/And ready/For whatever comes." These poems are timely for me. To watch how she remains buoyant despite our planet's distress. To avoid "the vicious nonchalance/Of being barely there." I trust her judgment because the poems distill not just the "honeyed lure of culture," but also rage. Together, they illuminate a path, "Searching the horizon/For some small sight/Of understanding."

The Island of Hvar

There is a square
Not like Trafalgar.
This one
Has a polished stone floor,
Smooth as historic fantasy,
That ties it to the centuries
Unnoticed by the coffee-sippers
Sitting on its sides.
Also a soccer ball is savaged
And the shouts of children
Fill the air.
My childhood
Had the summer smells
Of wet lawns in dry air,
The midnight sounds
Of train whistles
Carrying the future.
Differences:
What is it like
To grow up
With such an ancient public space
Embalmed with balmy island air
And no cars anywhere?
Is childhood shaped by architecture?
Tidy rows of porched brick houses,
Farm yards, tower blocks, suburban cul-de-sacs
And childhood
Never leaves these shapes
Of early play

They're here today
With me
In all the seasons
Of my memory.
Consciousness
Is such a shocking
Natural development.
What needed it
With all the rocks and trees and water,
Even after fins and wings, and limbs and noises?
Extraordinary
Knowing where you are
And where you've been
And what might come along
If one can get away from oneself
In the world
And think about these spaces
That shaped our lives
And circumscribed our growth.
What might have been
If we had been
At play
In any way
In one of these
We see today
As travelers.

27 November – 13 December 2018

The Wondrous Perception of Waves

The lizard
Crawled out of the sea
Still gooey inside.
It needed
Scales
To protect its soft flesh,
Smell
For safe food
Or bad bogs –
Occasional perfume.
It needed
To hear
Approaching enemies
Or tasty bugs to eat.
And certainly
It needed to see
The glories
Given by the light.
All this was hard work
So it needed to sleep
Perchance to dream.
And thus comes
Consciousness –
Constant awarenesses
Of where we are
In all these waves
Of sound and sight and smell.
And thus the need
The preciousness
And sweet release
Of sleep.

2 April 2021

Grief

Grief
Laps
At the tied-up end of day
And is there again
Slapping at the sides
In the open-eyed
First morning sun.
The surges have retreated
With the dull lull
Of stormless weather.
But the longing
Continues
Unabated
Unsatisfied
Searching the horizon
For some small sight
Of understanding.

July – August 2020

Death by Oyster

Could anyone ever object to a tree?
To the meanest of streets
It brings its blessings.
Grim London grows its bearability
In gardens –
Lined up in little rows
Behind the touching intimacy
Of brick-faced houses;
Or spreading out and flowering
In squares and frequent parks.
Its future folly flawed
Springs up in sterile steel and glass
And disconnects Great London
From its past.
And yet we flourish here
Like bees besotted
With the hectic hive.
What does it mean to me,
To want to be this much alive
Now that defining details
Of my plot
Are long-past sown
And I am free to reap
And mostly on my own?
I could retire bucolically
And linger quietly
In some dull Stygian hole
Were not experience
The utmost goal.

When visitors arrive
They want to walk
Or sit in parks
Or shop or eat and drink.
I am surprised
Because, for me, for nourishment
The honeyed lure of culture
Sets my course
And drives me on like drought.
The convoluted maps that get me there,
The buses, bridges, shops,
The conflagration of the streets
The buzzing busy hordes
A burgeoning complexity –
A swarm –
A blooming love affair!
I recently was warned off eating oysters raw.
Ah, death by oyster!
After all of this
Just more delight.
Oh, bring it on!

5 September 2015

The Voice of the Buses

Since the window at night
With the lights off
Has become so important
For looking out at the bus stop
To see if anyone is moving about
Out there,
The leaves have opened out
Into a confusing wind dance
And all that is left
Is the voice of the buses
Passing by
And not stopping.

12 April 2020

Being

With waves
Of sound
Of light
Of smell
We come to know the world.
The tides
Of gassy breath
Are how we touch,
Exchange, belong,
To all the other
Molecules.
The gutty depth
That plummets
Through emotion
Sounds the ocean
Of response.
But nothing
Even from the raft of thought
Accounts for consciousness.

9 May 2010

Positively

When I am worrying
In search of sleep
I wander
To the rolling of the ship
Through icy oceans of Antarctica
Or think about the chance
To stand upon the sandy crossroads
Of Uzbekistan
And ponder Alexander.
I contemplate
The married couple and their friends
Who spend "Another Year"
Against the couple who unravel
In "Blue Valentine."
I glory
In the little man
Who has within
One quarter from my genes;
Appreciate
St. Stephens Walbrook near to Mansion House,
And Mahler's 6th by ALL the orchestras,
Monet, Vermeer, Cezanne and Rothko,
All the lilacs, candlelight, asparagus and silver
From past dinners with good friends.
But when in wandering
I come upon the old woman
Hunched in saffron, violet and yellow,
Against the white-washed walls,
Walking ceaselessly
And spinning

All the prayer wheels
Of that ancient temple in Bhutan,
I hope that I will
Wonder ceaselessly
About the nature of HER need.

5 March 2011

On My Rounds

Such a difference
Life behind
Closed drapes,
Shaded in
Interior isolation only.
The walls
And furnishings
Of shutting out
The world outside,
Which is available continuously
To windows
Widely open:
Trees
And roads
And changing skies
Birdsong and street chatter
And all things tempting
Going on out there
But mainly
Something other than the self.

19 April 2020

Aftermath

Such a clean month
January;
The *fol de rol*
All gone
To fallow memory;
The light
Fighting its way back;
The wind-seared streets
Shining
With a lack of lies.

12 January 2012

On the Death of Seamus Heaney

"As is the generation of leaves"
So says Homer
"Mankind –
When one falls
Another never fails to take its place."
Appropriately,
Outside the window
Leaves are turning dry,
And a great poet
Is gone from this world.
Autumn has always been
The sweetest,
Crisp with regret
For failing summer,
Pungent with a sharp urgency of light
Before the fall's diminishment.
I, too, grow old
In this now suitable sweetness.
But I have dared to eat a million peaches
By a million moons
Full with the fertile promise
Of summer's wild abundance
That is waning now.
Yet filling in the darkness
Is a welling of experience
As fearless
As the riot of bright leaves
That rage
Before their journey to the earth.

2 September 2013

History

Time,
Being motion through space,
Most of our
Movements
Through the spaces
Of our lives
Are relatively insignificant.
But sometimes
We slip into history
With a substantial jolt:
Where you were,
When Kennedy died,
Or Princess Diana,
What you saw
In San Francisco,
When the Earth quaked,
Or witnessed
Of the crumbling towers.
So now this:
The making very near
And small
Of our activities.
We're plagued by fear
Of other people:
Joggers spraying sweat and germs,
Youthful arrogance,
Jostlers in a queue,
Or grabbers for the Standard news
Impatiently too close

And sneering at the old.
But being here
In these extraordinary times
When the kaleidoscope of culture
Myriad and various
Delights of taste and sound and sight
— LONDON —
Silenced
To everything
But walks along the river
Through the blooming park,
And friends,
Crucially: AND FRIENDS.
How we stayed together
Moving through these times,
A chain of isolated links.
Even Homer might have said of us
Things of song
For men of the future!

16 April – 13 May

Eclipse

What to offer Artemis
After the eclipse?
It must be something precious, personal:
My two pound coins?
Their deathly metal taste
Not suitable.
Oysters, roses?
Soft melons, sweet berries?
No animal will satisfy
A goddess who reveres them all.
Perhaps this poem will qualify,
Fulfill that promise
That I made the day
She granted that the clouds parted
So we saw
In all the naked newness
Of her full absence
The way she stood
Astride the sun,
The veritable sun
And blocked its light.
We privileged few
Permitted to observe
Her perfect power
Ringed with fire,
Bringing blackness to a startled world,
Unleashing disarray and disbelief
As is her usual wont,
Goddess of fertility.

Remember that I howled
With such delight that morning and
Accept this, then,
My offering of thanks
For gracing us
With such a gift.

July – December 2009

For Nina
Clutter

The urge in me
Is for protection,
Nurture, preservation.
Never one room
With a low table
And a single vase.
Ticket stubs
And dying plants
Travel trophies
Days old chicken
Dried and fading flowers
Every greeting card
And long gone calendar
Receipts and
Shoes and clothes
From decades passed.
Every object in this house
Has a story
Or a place
From which it came;
Every essence has its use,
Imagined future purpose,
Waste forbidden.
A lifetime of stuff,
The heir's despair,
The stuff of a lifetime
Gathering dust.

But when one wanders
At dusk
Through "half deserted streets"
And wonders
As the lights come on:
The variegated multitudes
Of self expression
Behind the windows,
Galaxies of domesticity
Constellations of the intimate.
Home is still
A mainly private place
And how we fill it
So much more than
Decoration
Or condition psychological –
Celebration
Of what we value
Who we are
What we like to see
Around us,
Comfort quotidian
Pleasure aesthetic
Memories preserved.
The cave of the wizard
Is not bare
And how can anyone
Make judgements
On what's there.

8 December 2019

All Change

The world seemed destined
Anyway
For solitude:
A single room
Or even several,
Devices everywhere
Work from home
Food delivered
On-line orders
No need to ever go outside
The Great God Amazon.
Now this virus –
Mother Nature culling –
Finishes the job.
How will they ever meet
Or marry
Or have children?
Logical solution
To too many people
Connected so much more now
Electronically
In isolation.

22 March 2020

Haiku Not

The six or seven
Lovely scarlet leaves
Left on the trees
Tossing in the wind.
The three quarter moon
Managing to break free
Of the torrential clouds.
The drapery
Of Geraldine Walther's
Palazzo trousers
As she played
The Bartok Quartets
In Berkeley.

7 December 2019

Fulfillment

What did Clytaemnestra do
After she killed the S.O.B.
(Her life not really being over
Despite all curses to the contrary?)
Weaving wasn't
How she saw herself
As solitude set in;
No poets sang to her
Around the fire
To arm her hours
Against such darkness.
Most certainly her children –
The ones remaining –
Had moved on.
No nurturer,
Perhaps she tried
To turn to gardening.
Some knew,
Perhaps she learned,
That most plants
Want their flowers cut
For clearing out old growths
However powerful their beauty
Or their strength.
Slash now
Or once they fade,
It matters not,
The next need spaces
For their bursting forth.

Thus vases
Full of blooms
Do not demand a penance
When they grace our rooms,
And hours scorched with sun
And glittering with guilt
May, over time,
Be brought to bear
With faint refrain of healing,
Which might grow within her
While she waited
For her final destiny:
As denizen of demise.

22 May 2009

A Houseguest in
San Cassiano

I sat
In springtime Tuscan sun
Before the ancient church
Which looked more Celtic
Than the Romanesque.
The doors were locked
But I could hear
An organist at work
And I was patient –
Not hard to be
On such a lovely afternoon.
It gave me time
To ponder all my failings:
Excess of
Opinions, salumi, red wine;
A lack of
Quietude, political acuity, organic food.
Too fat, too urban, too naïve
Or jaded;
Too much into clothes and too unfit.
Tumbling out they came
And down the smoky mountainside
They went
Awaiting absolution
From the still-locked church.

12 March 2012

Metamorphical Musings

There is a limitless variety
Of change.
When the seasons
Come and go
Almost unopposed
Their flow
Is natural.
And as we age
The change
Is imperceptible
Until that sudden shock
When it is not.
Experience
Is also change:
The sound of symphonies,
A patch within a perfect work of art,
A brilliant word of dialogue
Or twist of plot,
A column Byzantine,
Tibetan Temple
Where the Dalai Lama
Left an imprint in his bed,
Antarctic Ice,
Even the Higgs boson.
Himalayan vista,
Ocean beach,
Quiet forest trail,
Eclipse totality –
A London alleyway
That leads into an unknown antique church,
But here
A different kind of change

Is also underway:
The shops that come and go,
The thousand cranes
That change a city
From its well-constructed myth
Of stone and wooden monuments
And once-imagined permanence
Into the modern canyons –
Glass and steel
That are the future global style
To house
The way too many people in the world.
This change is hardest
Defined as we might be
By these perceptions of surroundings
As a frozen expectation
Of quotidian utility.
As it slips away
We contemplate our own
And so we must.
Acceptance
Of the moving on of things
A blessed alternative
To a demise
Of unappreciated catastrophic suddenness.
Ebb and flow
Two steps forward
One behind,
These dogs will have their day,
But we will triumph on
And fill our cups
With all we can
However long we may.

11 September 2017

Dimensions:
Kronos Quartet

The music
Of a string quartet
Filled the hall
Submerging all:
A universe of sound.
In search of flame
From where –
What plane –
That frantic moth
Entered the wall
Of stunning waves?
Then,
Of what
Was it aware
After?

9 October 2011

At Troy

Καὶ ανθρώποισι
    εσσομένοισι

There's still a hill
A citadel
At Ilium
And Homer
Is as real
As any mind
Can find him,
Recreated
Every time he's read.
It's he
Has made those heroes
Live through time
Helen's sluttishness
Is his
Not hers.
Indeed the power of his song
Has guaranteed her immortality,
Such as it is.
But only
Stones
Small, stunted trees
And sky
Are what endure
The raging waves of wind invisible
At Troy.
Many times

In layered space of land
A human hand
Placed stones deliberately
And set the trees
That now withstanding stand
Somehow,
As once their unknown makers were,
Sustained,
Above the sorrowful and timeless plain,
And here, for me, today remain
Man of the future come to see his song.

8 July 1999

For John Searle

That Extra Cup of Coffee in the Morning

The undeniablity
Of the determined and expanding
Sub-atomic universe
Is like the ripples
On a lake
Into which
A stone
Has been thrown.
Free will –
The unpredictability –
Is like a random leaf
Floating on the surface.
Its fall
Is also
Pre-determined
But not precisely
Where
It will disturb
The ripples.
And there's the rub –
The small
Within the great –
That gives each life
Its choice
Within its weighty fate.

26 September 2014

The London Poems

PART ONE

She's like a cat
That girl.
Her eyes
Glaze with artifice
As she tries to disguise
Her accent –
Working class –
And she pretends
That playing
The important part
Of Salon Assistant
Comes naturally
Gracefully.
All the while
She watches herself
In the mirrors:
Her perfect makeup
The sleekness
Of her shining hair.

19 March 2013

For Judy

"I'm jealous"
She said
"You are surrounded
By such beauty
And I've become
So bitter"
But I have worked at beauty
All my life –
If love is the point
Of being alive
Then admiring beauty
Is a part of it.
It's mostly about nature
Seeing something each day
Arresting:
Movement, breath
Or disbelief –
The thief of wonder –
Only briefly
A moment or two
But every day.
The sound of an owl,
A flaming tree
Hurried along by the impatient wind
For the demise of leaves,
The smell of lilacs,
Coffee, rain,
The taste of oysters raw, or chocolate.
And there are choices,

What one puts on walls and shelves
Preserving memories
Of places traveled and people loved,
Also informed by decades spent
In looking at great art.
Out of what receptacle
Does one sip the wine or tea
Or eat the food
Which has its own appeal?
It's certainly not hard
To open up the senses
To nourishment.
It's everywhere –
Beauty –
So, did you notice
The bright full moon
Rising in the sky
Last night?

30 November – 9 December 2020

Fall

The leaves are thinning
Like hair
Unaware
It's going old
And in the air
A slash of cold
Quickening
And slightly sad
As summer slips away
Like Eliot's cat
Slinking secretly
And sly
Into memory.

3 September 2011

The Cruelest Month

Nothing happened
In April this year.
The diary is blank.
Theatres were dark,
Holidays cancelled,
No sports events
Or pub dissections afterwards,
No art was looked at
On the canvas,
No meals were shared
With friends
In special settings.
What happened,
Other than
Too many people died,
Was pretty much inside
And quiet.
And all the walks
Extended past necessity
And lengthened
Into further explorations
Of long neglected local treasures,
Observations purposeless,
Now noted lovingly
Just as the light itself
Was lingering
And stretching into spring

27 April 2020

Getting On With It or Don't Blame the Folks

ANTIGONE:
The Gods decreed that you would do these deeds.

OEDIPUS:
I had FREE WILL. I made the choices:
FIGHT AND MARRY.

ANTIGONE:
BUT YOU DIDN'T KNOW.....

OEDIPUS:
WE NEVER KNOW what we are born into.
And luckier than most, I was informed. It's why
I left my home.

ANTIGONE:
PRE-DETERMINED and not fair, that you
should suffer.

OEDIPUS:
Now that I know what's been fulfilled,
I'm free to be MYSELF!

ANTIGONE:
But you are BLIND!

OEDIPUS:
Only WITHOUT, WITHIN I see and it has
made me WHOLE. I've left the past.
I am my OWN, at last.

9 March 2012

Disqualified Doors

Disqualified doors
One in the Physic Garden
One near Red Lion Square
Disabled
Not where they've opened before.
Both had possible alternatives
So redirection:
Quanta
Changing course.
If existence
Is only interaction
What is choice?
Free Will?
And what results
From choosing
Incorrectly?

7 September 2022

Christmas Wife

I decorate
Against the darkness,
Make things beautiful
And fine
Because there is a joy
And peace and calm
In things well done.
In solitude
The mortal fight
Against the dead of winter
Satisfies.
But still,
On this year's tree
There's one bare spot
Too high to reach
To hang the ornament
Which would be perfect there.
I've come to terms
With imperfection.
It's glorious life's reminder
Of potential wound –
The parenthetical husband –
Signed at the end
Of Christmas letters
Because he's given over
All his life to booze and isn't there:
A spot that's bare,
Damaged at the top
And now unreachable.

25 December 2006

A Waking Moan

To morning moon
A brilliant morn
Awaits me soon

13 September 2011

Ending

He settled into sloth
As one sinking into a warm bath.
He let his hair grow long
But it was stringy as leftovers.
What was once
A bright crystal lens in him
Clouded over with stubbornness.
And he never noticed
When his wife went.

2011

Exile

Real Tibetan monks
Now from India
In red and gold
Assemble
In two outward-angling rows
Upon a decorated stage
In Berkeley.
Their frog-throated chanting
Sounds like horns,
Like ancient rhythmic secrets,
Like the wind
Roaring through
An icy mountain pass
Too high for breath.
With cymbals, horns and bells
Four turquoise drums
Summon in the sound
In burgundy and saffron –
Monotony refreshed, recalled;
A ritual needing no translation into trance:
The beat of breath, of waves;
The sigh of wind.
Afterwards we learn
A grateful Mickey Hart is in the audience
And thanked, among others,
By a small monk
From San Jose
Who comes forward to announce
That to see the Dalai Lama
Next month
We need to phone
The Ticket Master.

15 March 2007

Argonautica

Medea,
Unlike Jason,
Not the perfect person.
Passion
Like an arrow
Did destroy her – almost –
First betraying father, brothers,
For him,
Then betrayed, in turn,
By him.
Still, she changed her role,
Refusing to be victim.
She willed
Destruction
of the Fruit
Of Passion,
Left no trace
To trip her later.
And once done
Forgotten witchiness regained,
Control preferred
To Passion's fleeting Paradise,
That flips to Poison,
And, like Fleece,
Once captured,
Is discarded
But not without its cost.

9 December 2007

Dust

Each man is an island
A solitary lens
Re-interpreting and disturbing
What it sees
From its promontory
Of the self.
That bowl of peaches
Is a fact
But no two painters
Render it the same
Not even when all art
Was meant to be anonymous.
All of us
Sing a poem (or a rage)
Into the universe
And add
Unknown dimensions
Of our own –
Our consciousness –
To what is merely matter.
Incomplete it is,
Without each solitary speck
Of individual voice
To fathom deeper
Than did matter:
Art.

1 January 2008

Old Ladies

Old Ladies
Aren't they lovely?
Some wear black
And others yellow
Some play bridge
And others knit
Tai Chi in China
In Greece they sit
On hillsides in the sun
(The old men
Drinking in the town.)
Many pray
In churches, mosques and temples,
Some in pews
And others walking with their beads.
Some must do it secretly,
While others laugh together
Over tea or walks
Or while they cook.
They read in groups
And sing in choirs
Tend their gardens
And grandchildren.
In India Italy Japan
In Canada Uzbekistan Bhutan
Old Ladies
On this we can agree
Old Ladies when they come together
They are free.

9 January 2022

In Bhutan

That woman
In Bhutan
Old, hunched
Swinging her beads
She was walking
Around the white-painted temple
Dressed in fuschia, scarlet and yellow.
Over and over
Around and around
Incanting the prayers.
Her life.
Mine.

3 August 2019

Summer in London

Somehow
June just slipped in
And summer was here.
It was as though
It was never expected
Yet here it was,
Trees full
And lush
And green
And swaying in the sun,
No longer able to see
Across the road
Through skeletal branches
Beyond the window.
The Vermeer poster
I have on my wall
Is part of my life:
The painter
With his back to me
The chequered floor.
There is a round circle
Of paler grey
Right beneath
The woman's trumpet
That's part
Of my waking up
Each day
In this finely-arrived summer.
The trees

Dance outside the window
And I wonder
Who
Would ever be interested
In the book
I could write
About
This London that I love

12 June 2022

3:06 16/10/2017

At this moment in time
A hurricane is approaching Ireland
Fire is destroying Northern California
Burma's Moslems are learning evil
Mexico is in ruins
Somalis are mourning exploding bodies
Puerto Rico is forgotten
Ego consumes the US President
The Brits are on the road to disaster
The Arab world is destroying itself
The Chinese are immune to all of this
The sky has turned an alarming shade of yellow
And I am about to take a bath.

16 October 2017

GRAECIA ANTIQUA

What do the old men do
To fill quotidian time
To give it substance,
Stronger currents having passed them by
And harnessed for a younger crew
Much tougher,
Sweating towards a future relevance?

These guys,
Unlike their housebound wives
Whose heavy worn out lives
Appear on solitary doorsteps
Kerchiefed in a darkened room
All bundled up against the sun's assault
Occasionally calling to each other
Overlooked
Across the rocky hillside paths.

These guys
Have found the grace
Of common hours
Clustered in a small cafe
Mostly silent
Mostly soothed by something sipped
At reverential pace
But most importantly
Together in a shared defense
Against the vicious nonchalance
Of being barely there.

Might we all
Wind out our threads
In such an intermingled way
Continuing our sweet surprise
At how we happen to each other
And might we share
Some of that solidness
Of old Greek men
In caps and coats
And cafe chairs.

13 August 2001

Eurydice's Choice

Orpheus - it's not his story;
After all, she's the one who dies.
In his favor
He's a man obsessed with love
Not power, riches, fame –
Perhaps with song.
But what could make her choose to stay
Reject the chaos of the light above
Reject the power of his love?
For Orpheus is not observed by her.
What does she find down there
Among the dust and whispers
Wandering in Elysium?
Does she discover pomegranates
Seeded in a virgin moon?
Or is it sudden stillness
Absence of the tumult,
Stuck down there
In shadowed corridors with shades.
Did she tire of pushing rocks of air up hills of lung?
That odd and even, black and white exchange
That all things breathing share,
The casting off and taking in –
One locus where
We living meet the rest of what is there
And touch.
Wing-footed Hermes
Leading each a different tour,
What words did he impart

What promises that guided her
Once Charon finished ferrying?
When Mephistopheles is shot
From place to place
He has to feel the walls
To find out where he is
And that's his hell,
As Marlowe says
"Everywhere but where He is."
It could mean peace
Freedom from the constant pull of other,
No place or sound or sight
Not even smell to stop the stillness.
It was her choice, you see,
To stumble, cough, cry out -
To stop that passage back
Into the dazzling riot that is life.
She chose release
And left him there
Bereft with loss
Equipped with Art
Immortally alone.

December 2004 / January 2005

Taking Stock

Autumn
Is illuminating
All the secret corners
Of the cupboard
That I call
My memory.
The light floods in,
Not April cruel
But thick and rich
A golden honey
Sweet with longing
Lurking in the nooks
Looking for the past.
It opens cracks
So suddenly
A flurry of dazed moths
Comes tumbling out.

My father told me
Once when I was very young
The shadowed light
That played across the wall
Was fairies dancing.
I have not forgot.
Perhaps it is the poignancy
Of seasons
With their tastes of change
That brings this summing up
And random inventory:

Flaming loss of leaves
Proximity of winter's mortal chill,
Uncertainty of spring.
My shelves are full,
Stocked with experience
Bought with choices
And ready
For whatever comes.

October/November 2011

London 2014

Is it not curious
To want to travel
Into history?
And is it there?
The streets still bear
The names
Marshalsea and Sawyer
Copperfield, Hanover Square.
And, once, there were
The handmade worlds
Of horsecarts, stalls and smells,
Fired and candle-lit but cold as well
Such pitiful extremes
Of desperate souls
On cobbled streets of brick and mud
All bonneted and booted
And unfair.
And where
Are we?
If you come now
Don't look for Dickens here,
What will appear,
While whizzing past on buses,
Is all made of glass and steel,
Cemented vertically
And sanitized
Into a way
Of dealing with today.
This city

Has a life force of its own
And breathes and flows
Discards and grows
And waits for no man.
Keats and Turner
Wollstonecraft
All breathed this air
Shakespeare and Milton
Handel, Pepys
A pint or two perhaps
And left genetic trace?
Their works remain
Inhabiting a country
Only of the brain.
Even The Tower,
Stolid as it stands
Floodlit at night,
Is still become a part of now.
So speedy is the change
That as the wrecking ball is done
We can't remember what it was
That stood before and now is gone.
We come for history
And fail to see
That we are making and a part
Of what is now and yet to be.

10 September 2014

For Chandler

My Angel Can't Fly

An angel with one wing
Still sings
Perhaps more soulfully.
Or one who doesn't fly
May ground itself
In something more sublime
And stumbling
Might even wander,
Singing tales of wars
Fought long ago,
Using memory
To get it right.
What is expected of angels?
And what wearies them?
The gods became petty
From immortal indolence
The arrogance and insolence of it
When given all our gifts.
Might angels long?
Perfection
The weight of which is ruin
Or even perfect peace,
For me, are not right probable.
The shutting off
Of all desire
The calming
Of all will.
Tame not

The wildness of my mind
At least not yet.
So much is left
To dazzle and engage
And endless things to learn
Along the curious and peerless path
I choose to suffer still:
This striving on
To know
Why fallen angels
Thrill.

October 2002

Transport

There are chartreuse camels
On the Fulham Road
And furniture
That is not faux
And the bus roars past
As though there were
Nothing at all to see there
Not even diners
In candlelit windows,
Or people dying of cancer
In the Royal Marsden Hospital.

August, 2010

Experience

To be
In this world
(As the Afghan movie says)
Means more
Than simple spheres
Of local life
Breathing air
Getting by
Hunting dreams
Of desperate acquisition,
Or obese feasts and dulling noise
Unflavored by a depth of vision,
Squandering spice and sight and sound.
Assuming
Roof and food and health and peace
Are not blessings
But are rights
Then what remains
Is filling up
The cup
Of ponder,
Turning toil
To meaning,
Trawling with a net
That widens
To the splendor
Of the world.
Name words
Know play

Dance art
Grow thought
Make work,
Form home
Its shape and space.
And what it means
To be a traveler
Or not to be a traveler.

If it's a path
Then we should wander
On it
Through the forests, seas and stars
The chemistries, psychologies
The symphonies and politics
And lily ponds and madeleines
And temples and philosophies and myths.
Poverty is lacking this –
Shared airy stuff of concept
Outside time.

But then
We should take to the road.
Rivers really are the same,
Each rushing
Self-contained
From past to present, future
Resurrected water
All the same

In constant flow;
But the streets are not,
It takes days to learn the streets
At least three days and a good map
For each
And patience is the currency of wonder.

The shape and space
And meaning
Of thought work art
And home
And being alone
And on a different road,
The thrilling sense
Of strange.

"Things come in pairs
Eaters of meat are on the way out
Machines have made the world dirty"
The guide wears a cardigan and well cut slacks
I wear a tunic and trousers and shawl
A coming together
Of river and road and river.

Treasure
Slender wonder
Ponder splendor
Wander
Real fortune is only and all
Experience.

And people ask
Does India
Really shake the soul?
It is simply a shift
An axis tilt
It engulfs
Alone on a rooftop in Orcha
Or at the lakeside in Pushkar
It floats up
From the blue city
To the hilltop fort
At dusk
The sound of prayers
And cooking pots
And watery women's sighs
Griefs and joys
And viciousness
Unknowable
Coming to know
Always known
In stunning splendid clarity
The wonder and the rending
Of an opening,
A moment
In this world.

14 March 04

For Oliver Ulash and Ezra

Update

It is
An evening in early February
And I am sitting
In a room that has been mine
For almost fifty years
Watching the dreary dwindling
Of the evening's light.
Embedded in these walls
Are many memories
And much growth.
But change
Is not helpful
For the old.
The daily surprise
Of being alive
Is such a treasure!
And even better yet
That I might grow
A measure.
I send into
What's left
A wish
That I might make it so.

5 February 2023